MULTIPLE MEANINGS OF LIFE

DRUG ABUSE

S.F.GEELANI

The drug is not a dangerous substance itself. But people misuse it in many ways. It is highly dangerous and can cause serious health problems if one takes it on a regular basis. The drug has become a trend in today's world. Today's generation has become obsessed with following whatever is new or trending in the world. Such is the situation in case of drugs.

"Your decision to kill your addiction will become a reality only if you believe and reinforce the fact that you have the capacity to do it.""Your decision to kill your addiction will become a reality only if you believe and reinforce the fact that you have the capacity to do it."

Author S.F.Geelani

Contents

Preface

This book is my second book. In the first book (Eternal Soul), I tried to show the fact that no one love you more than your family and just focus upon your goals and dreams.

The idea for this book came to me after viewing my friend who was involved in drug activities, and because of that I lost my friend.

My goal in writing this book is for people to read it and turn away from the things that can ruin their lives and the lives of their loved ones. We should stay away from drugs as much as possible and tell others about it. And all the organisations these days that are working to eliminate drugs, we should support them as well.

Acknowledgements

I wish a grateful and pleasurable acknowledgement, my deep gratitude to My father, Syed Muzamil Geelani and my mother, Shamshada Akhter. For their constant support and encouragement and taught me the different meaning of Life. And taught me the difference between human being and being human.

I am thankful to Mr Moh Siddiq Mir, and Mr Reyaz Ul Gani Wani, for critical reviews of the text. I thank Aarif Hussain Kuchay for his tangible, but always unspoken support, for this book.

I am also very thankful to the whole staff of my old school, Army Goodwill Public School pahalgam, for encouraging me...

Syed Muzamil Geelani

Prologue

Hello, My name is Tony & I'm a doctor.

Let me narrate a story of my best friend James, who gets involved in bad activities, and because of that, I lost him.

James is my childhood friend, & we started our journey with each other.

James belongs to a very Rich family & I belong to a Middle-class family.

I wanted to become a doctor, but my family was not financially well. My friend James, always financially helps me because he knows everything about my family's condition, & he also wanted to see me become a doctor.

In college life, together we enjoyed very special moments, and during those days my friend got involved in bad activities but I was not aware about it, as he does not want to share It with me.

CHAPTER ONE

One day I & my best friend James went on a trip to Goa. On the way he stopped the car and told me, wait a moment I will go to the washroom and he went towards the washroom.

After 30 minutes, I was waiting in the car, but he never came and I got worried about him. I tried to call, but he dropped the call.

Being worried I decided to search for him, and I went to search. Firstly I went to the washroom but he was not there.

I searched everywhere. After a while, he called me and said where are you? I'm waiting in the car.

I replied I'm searching for you in every place where you have been? I was worried about you.

In reply, He told me to come in the car and I will tell you everything.

When I reached the car, I told him now you tell me where you were and he said actually, Suddenly I remembered some important work So I was going to finish the work.

When I heard this, I said that If you had work, you should have told me and I would have accompanied you.

After that, he told me sorry, Started the car and we started our journey again.

Around 11'o o'clock we reached a deserted place, and no one was seen here from afar. Walking a little further, we saw a hotel and we decided to spend the night in the hotel.

When we entered the hotel, we saw that an old man was sleeping on a chair.

We went to the old man and tried to wake him up.

When this old man woke up, we asked him if any room was available.

He replied that no one has been here for a long time. Yes, all the rooms are empty.

When we heard this, I got scared and I told my friend that I think this is a haunted house.

He said don't be afraid of ghosts, ghosts do not exist in the real world.

And that old man told us, Come with me, I will show you a Room, It made a lot of noise when we walked down the stairs behind the old man.

When we reached the Room we saw it was a very beautiful room, and we decided to stay in the room.

After dinner, I got a lot of sleep and I slept peacefully.

When I was asleep James took drugs and after taking drugs he saw some creatures and he began to shout, and when I heard his voice, I woke up asleep. And I quickly went to him. When I reached, I saw that he was very scared.

And I asked what happened?

He told me that I saw a strange creature in my bed.

I told him that there is no such thing here, this is your delusion.

And I told him don't think about that and try to sleep.

I know there were other creatures here but I didn't tell him, because I thought that if I told him this, he would be even more frightened. And I fell asleep thinking all this.

The next day, after breakfast we were ready to start our journey again.

On the way, we enjoyed a lot. Finally, we reached Goa, and first, we went to the hotel room.

After some time we were ready to go towards Goa beach and when we reached Goa beach we saw very beautiful nature and people around the beach.

My friend and I first did water gliding. After we finished gliding we started to play with sand and water like small kids, because at that time we remember our childhood days.

After a while, taking some rest he told me that I have some kind of work so I will go to finish it.

Then I said to him," I will go with you and Maybe you will need my help."

When I said this to him, he told me, don't worry I will handle that. And he said that if I need your help, I will call you.

After saying this, he left me in the room and then goes out

observing all this, I thought that my friend was hiding something from me.

Then I thought he would be in some kind of problem and he is hiding his problem from me Because he didn't want to give me tension.

Now I have decided that when he came into the room I will ask him about it.

Actually, he ran out of drugs and went to get drugs. And that's why he lied to me. He searched for drugs everywhere but found no drugs. While searching, he approached whom he talked about drugs.

The man then took him to a drug dealer And told everything to him.

The drug dealer got suspicious about James and thought that he was sent by the police to arrest us all.

And he said to his people to beat James. And They beat him too much.

James said, " I'm not a policeman, please trust me. I ran out of drugs, that is why I came here".

When the drug dealer heard all this, he believed James' words And told his companions to leave him and give him some drugs.

James got very happy when he heard about drugs and he forgot his pains and only thought about drugs.

After taking drugs he returned to the hotel room, and I got scared when I saw him because his whole body was bleeding.

I gave him some medicine and water, then asked him what happened to you? He told me that on my way back to the hotel I met some thieves and they told me to give us what you have. They snatched everything from me but I did not give them my phone and I told them to take everything but not my phone.

On hearing this, they all started beating me, and meanwhile, the police came there and arrested them.

Listening to James, I was convinced that my friend was hiding something from me, and I decided that now I will find out for myself what my friend is hiding from me.

He knew, he was doing wrong by hiding it from me, but he was afraid that if I found out, I would end our friendship.

He loved me so much and he didn't want to lose me, Nor did I want to lose James.

CHAPTER TWO

The next day, In the morning James goes to the bathroom and suddenly his mouth started bleeding. James understood that this is all due to my high dose of drugs. And he thinks that now I will not survive.

Meanwhile, I went to the bathroom. When James sees me, he hides his face and leaves without telling me.

After that when I looked into the washbasin I saw some blood stains in the washbasin. I was very scared to see this, and I got out of the washroom and asked James about it.

And he told me that when I was shaving, my face was cut a little, and the same blood remained in the washbasin.

I understood that James is lying to me, so I told him, brother, you have been hiding something from me since we came to Goa.

Please tell me, what is it that you cannot share with me?

In response, he angrily told me that it is not necessary to tell you everything, and he said that ever since we came here, you have been asking question after question.

He vents all his anger on me and then left.

When I heard all this, tears started coming to my eyes and I cried a lot because James had never spoken to me like that before.

It hurt me a lot and I went and sat alone on the beachside, but I also had in mind that my friend would come to me to apologize.

On the other hand, James went for a walk to adjust his temper.

On the way, he thought about the same incident and felt guilty.

In fact, James didn't really know what he had actually done.

He was getting angry at the little things and his behavior was also changing, all because of taking drugs.

And when he felt guilty, he took large quantities of drugs and began to cross the road, and in the meanwhile, he met with an accident.

I still do not know that James met with an accident and I am waiting for him to come to me and say sorry to me.

After a while, I got a call from James' number but I didn't pick up the call. Because I think my friend would apologize, and I don't want him to apologize like that, I want him to come and take me with him.

After that, some unknown person called on my phone and I picked up the call. When I picked up the call, he told me that your friend, James, had an accident, and he said that I will send you the location on your number, you come quickly.

When I heard all this, I got very scared and reached away at its sent location.

I saw that there is a lot of crowd around James but none of them help him, they just take pictures and videos with him.

I hurried off and put James' head on my lap and told the people that, you don't see this man dying on the street here. You all should have helped him but you are all only taking pictures and videos.

Then one of the person said that we don't all want to get involved in a police case nor do we all want the police to think that one of us is the culprit. *(A good person is one who, when sees someone in trouble, helps him without thinking about anything.)*

(The thing that is going on in our society today is that if we see someone in trouble, we doesn't help them because we don't want to get ourselves in trouble.)

After this scene, I thought that I can't waste too much time here, so I took James to the City hospital. As soon as I took him to the hospital, the doctors checked his condition and took him to the emergency ward.

I was even more frightened to see this and consider myself responsible for James' condition. Because I thought that if I wouldn't ask him anything, he wouldn't confront me and he wouldn't have an accident.

After some time, I was sitting out of the ward and thinking about James' condition. Meanwhile, the doctor came and I asked him, "Is my friend all right now?"

In response, he told me that actually, "I'm going to call the police, they will come and arrest your friend."

When I heard all this I was amazed and asked the doctor, "What happened, What has my friend done?"

In response, the doctor said that your friend is taking all kinds of drugs, and today your friend had taken a high dose of Cocaine.

If he takes it like this, it will be difficult for him to survive.

I can't believe it, when I heard this from the doctor and I said "No, my friend doesn't do all this, You must have had a misunderstanding."

After that, the Doctor showed me James' report card. When I saw the report, I got very shocked and started crying, and then pleaded with the doctor not to tell this thing to anyone else.

When the doctor saw my condition, he said, "OK, I won't tell anyone."

Then I said to the doctor, "Thank you very much."

Then the doctor left and I sat on the bench and started thinking about why my friend hide such a big thing from me, and then I decided that I would talk to James about it.

After a while, the doctor again came and told me that now your friend is all right, you can go now to see him, but be careful that your friend never take drugs again, because if he takes drugs again, he won't be safe.

After listening to the doctor, I ran to see James.

Arriving there, I hugged James tightly and started crying.

He got emotional when he saw me and said, "Brother, forgive me for everything I said."

Then I answered, "Brother, it's OK". I know you didn't do it on purpose." And I thought in my mind that it is not the right time to talk about what the doctor told me.

CHAPTER THREE

2 days later, James was discharged from the hospital and we were going to the hotel. Meanwhile, I said, "Brother, we have been here for a long time and now we should go back home."

In response, he said, "OK, we'll go home tomorrow."

Then I thought in my mind that I will not let James take drugs anymore and tomorrow I will go home and talk to him about drugs.The next morning, we were going Home. James was talking to me on the way but I didn't care what he said, because the only thing going on in my mind is how I will save my friend's life.

When James realized that I was thinking something, he asked me, "Brother, What are you thinking? Is everything fine?"

In response, I said, " Yes, brother, everything is fine."

Again he said, what were you thinking then.

I replied again and said nothing.

After that along the way we have a place to eat.

After eating food, blood started to flow from James' Mouth. And he gets up from the meal and runs to the washroom.

When I saw this, I chased after him and tried to look into the washroom window.

And I saw a lot of blood coming out of his mouth. Noticing this, I fell down there and started crying a lot.

On the other hand, James was also very scared and crying, he said to himself, "I will not survive."

And he wondered what will happen to my dear friend who has not done anything since I left this world. And then he decided that he'll do something that will make me start hating him because he wanted me to do something on my own.

After that, he came out of the washroom and saw me outside the washroom and he got very scared. He thought that he must have seen me doing all this, and in a hushed voice, he told me what you are doing here.

Then I said, "My foot slipped and I fell down."

On hearing this, he asked me if I was fine?
I said, "Yes I'm fine and I said it's getting late, we should go now."
We got out of there, and then we started our journey again.
On the way, we were talking about our childhood memories and missing the days when we were children.

We could not even imagine being separated from each other, but we did not know that fate would separate us.

And finally, we reached the house. I used to stay at James' house but today he told me to go home.

It hurt me a lot but I still don't want to go because I didn't want to leave James alone and I thought when I leave James alone he would take drugs.

James also felt bad for saying all this to me, but he also wanted me to start hating him so that I will do something for myself so that I don't need him.

And finally, James agreed and I stayed there. Then he thought that he would do something bad which made me hate him.

At night after taking meals he wanted to take drugs but I was with him so he could not take drugs.

And I also knew that he would take drugs when I fell asleep.

So that's why I didn't sleep unless James slept.

After a while, when I thought that he was asleep, then I slept as well.

But he was not sleeping, he was just acting like he was sleeping, and when he saw that I'm asleep, he left the room and went somewhere to get drugs.

The Next Day, in the morning, when I woke up, I saw that James was not there, so I searched for him everywhere in the house.

But I saw that he was not at home, so I went to Mr. Mathur.

Mr. Mathur is a rich businessman and he is the father of James.

I told him that James is not at home and I asked where he had gone.

Mr. Mathur asked me, who are you to ask about him and said, "I know you are with him because of money, tell me how much money you want but after that please leave him alone."

In response, I said to him, sir, you took it wrong, I was not with him because of money, I was with him because of our childhood friendship.

Then he said that I know everything about middle-class people, they trap rich people in their friendship and then rob them of their money, and after saying that, he left.

James' whole Family hates me because I belong to a middle-class family. His family always tells him not to be friends with me because they think I am his friend only because of money.

(This is what is happening in our society today, we look at a man's clothes and his money, and we judge how good he is.)

I don't mind Mr. Mathur's words, in fact, I don't care what people think of me, I just care what my friends think of me.

After that, I tried to call James but his phone turned off. I got very upset and I was convinced that he must have gone for drugs.

I called all my friends and asked about James, But they did not know where he had gone.

My friends and I searched for him everywhere but he was not found.

Then I decided to go to James' home and wait for him.

CHAPTER FOUR

It was evening but he had not come home yet.

And finally, he reached the house around 2 o'clock. I was amazed to see him because his clothes were full of blood, and I thought it was the right time to talk with him about Drugs'.

And I said to him, "I know brother, you get involved in bad activities, please brother give up all those things."

When James heard this, he was instantly shocked and said, ``What do you mean by bad activities? Can you explain properly?"

In response, I said that when your accident happened, the doctor did show your reports and told me everything.

I said, "Brother, I know everything but I didn't tell you because I thought in my mind that it's not the right time to tell you all these things."

After that James was shocked too much and said, "Thank God, you know, now I'm not going to take drugs from you secretly anymore, it means that now I will take drugs in front of you."

While talking about all these things, a white packet came out of his pocket, and he took that white packet on his hand's palm and tried to smell it.

When I saw this, I was intensely shocked and went to stop him.

But he didn't stop and started fighting with me. At that moment I snatched that packet from him and I saw that it was cocaine, then I threw it out of the window.

When James saw that I had thrown cocaine out of the window, he got very angry and slapped me.

It was as if he had gone mad at the time and the first time I saw him so angry.

Then he went out of the room and searched the same Cocaine packet around the window.

I was not sad because he slapped me, I was sad to see his condition.

All the things that the doctor told me got into my mind. I cried a lot and thought about how I could save my friend's life. Then I decided that my friend should be angry with me, hit me, or not talk to me but now I would not let him take drugs anymore.

Then I went to James and I started looking for that cocaine packet and I found it. I was about to take it in my hand and put it in my mouth.

Meanwhile, James saw this, he knocked it out of my hands and slapped me again, and said, "What are you going to do, are you crazy?"

In response, I told him, "If you can't see my life begin to be ruined, how can I?"

and I told him, "Brother, why are you ruining your life, think of your family, what will happen to them without you and what will I do without you."

He listened to me and said that when I don't take it, my head aches a lot, I get angry, I feel tense, and I can't stop myself from taking it.

And he said I was tired of it and trying to control it and now I promised I won't do it from today.

I was glad to hear all this from him.

I thought my friend will fulfill this promise too because he has fulfilled the promise he made to me till today so I thought he would fulfil this promise too

But James decided that if he will not give up drugs, he'll go away from my life because he thought that because of that my life will be ruined.

And then I took him to Room. After we reached the room, he told me, If I was happy because he promised me that now he wouldn't be taking drugs.

In response, I said, "Yes, brother, I'm so happy for you to leave these things, I can't see you destroying your life in front of my eyes, because you are my everything and without you my life is incomplete."

Hearing this, he also got emotional and said, "Brother, thank you, for loving me so much."

Then I said to him, "Thanks for what, you are not only my friend, you are my family."

All of a sudden I got a call from my family and they said "You have not come home, come home tomorrow for two days." By saying this, they cut off the call.

Then James asked me who was calling?

I told him everything that the family was saying.

In response he said, "Tomorrow you will go home to see your family and don't worry about me, I'm all right now."

I obeyed him but I also have the fear in my heart that my friend will break the promise he made to me.

After that, we really enjoyed that night.But I didn't know that I would never see my friend again after the night.

CHAPTER FIVE

The next morning, after eating, James told me that now you go home because your family is waiting at home. He hugged me and said, "Brother I will miss you a lot."

In response I said, "Me too, brother will miss you a lot, but don't worry I will come back soon."

At that time I couldn't understand what my friend was actually saying to me.

After that, I left James' home and went towards my home. On the way, I was really very happy because I thought that my friend left the drugs' addiction.

On the other hand, James knew that he would never forget the drugs' addiction, so he decided to go away from my life, and then he told his parents that I want to leave the country for some time.

Then his parents said to him, "What happened, why do you want to leave the country for some time?"

In reply, he said, "I no longer want to meet with Tony. That is the reason I want to leave the country."

When his parents heard these words from him, Mr. Mathur told him, "I won't ask what happened between the two of you, but I was glad, you listened to me and broke up Your friendship with him and added "OK, I'll book your ticket to America this evening."

Then James went to his room and started packing. While packing, he looked at our pictures and reminded all

the days we spent together from childhood till today and cried a lot.

In the evening at around 6 o'clock, when I finally reached my house, the family was very happy when they saw me, and my parents asked me, "How are you? and how is your friend?"

In reply, I said, "I'm fine and now James is fine too."

Then my mother enquired me, "What do you mean by now James is fine too, what happened first with him."

In response I said, "Nothing, he was just a little sick but now he is alright."

After that, my mother said, "Well, you must be hungry, So eat the meal first."

After eating, I went outside the house and called James but he didn't pick up my call, because he has a flight today and he is going to the airport.

When James did not answer my call, I became very tense.

After a while, I got an SMS from James' number and I was very happy but when I read the SMS I felt very bad and started crying because James had written in it, "Brother we will never meet again, I am going away from your life forever and ever because I don't want your life to be ruined like mine."

And he added, "I know brother, you worry for me but don't worry for me. I'm alright, don't try to search for me and just focus on your goals because I want you to become a doctor."

He continued, "I know brother, I'm doing wrong with you but I also don't want you to destroy your life because of me."

And he said in it, "I know you can't live without me and I also can't live without you but it is necessary for us to move away from each other. Your memories and your love will always be with me."

He also said, "Take care of yourself and please, forgive me for this."

When I read all this I lost my sense and fell down to my knees and started crying loudly and said in a loud voice, "Oh, my friend, how you can do this wrong with me and why did you take this wrong path."

When my family and my neighbors heard my voice they came to me and asked me what happened? They asked, "Why are you crying?"

At that time I was not mentally well, so I didn't say a word to them.

After that my family took me home and then asked me to tell us What happened to you?

But at that time I just said, "Please, come back my friend, don't leave me alone, I can't live without you."

When my family heard these words from me they understood that James told me something wrong which hurts me very much. Then my parents called on his number but his number was coming off.

After that my parents took my phone and checked it and they saw in it all his messages, and then asked me what happened between you and your friend? Why did he tell you such things?

When I didn't give any answer to my parents' questions then my parents realized that I was gone into depression

and they said to me you need some rest, so they took me to my bedroom, turned off the lights of my room, and went from there.

My parents also got upset about us.

And I couldn't sleep that night. I just thought about my friend and looked at the pictures on my phone in which my friend and I had a lot of fun.

CHAPTER SIX

The next morning, I told my parents that I was going to search for James in his home because I thought he would not leave me alone.

In response, my parents said, "Ok but we will also go with you."

I agreed, when we reached his home's gate his security guards didn't allow us to go inside. They said to us that James refused to allow Tony and his family inside the gate. But they lied to us that James told them not to allow me and my family inside. Actually, Mr. Mathur said this to the security guards.

After that, I tried very hard to go inside the gate but they didn't allow me.

I became very frustrated and started fighting with security guards, beat all of them and went inside the gate, and started calling James loudly.

When his family heard my voice, they all came outside, Mr. Mathur also came outside and said, "James is not at home and he doesn't want to meet you again."

When I heard this, I said to him, "please, sir, tell me where he is?"

In reply, he said that I didn't tell you where he had gone.

Meantime my parents came there, when Mr. Mathur saw my parents, he said, "Wow! your poor parents are also coming with you, actually, your whole family is cheaper, you all want only money and because of that, you are searching for my child."

And he also added that you all got lost out of my house, otherwise I will call the police.

When my parents heard this, they got scared and they said to me, "Son, please, go back home with us.

But I told them, "No, I will not go back home without resembling James."

Saying this, I went inside the house and the security guards tried to stop me but I didn't stop.

After that Mr. Mathur called the police and said that an unknown person forcibly came into my house and started beating my security Guards.

I searched everywhere for James in the home but he was never found, then I was sure that he was not at home, he had gone away from home.

Then the police arrived and Mr. Mathur told them, "This is the same man I had told you about, please arrest him."

My parents requested Mr. Mathur, to stop the police but he refused the request.

The police arrested me, seated me in a jeep, and took me to the police station. When we reached the police station, they inserted me into a lock-up.

After a while, one police officer and a few constables came into my lock-up. The police officer started an investigation. He asked me, "Why did you go to Mr. Mathur's house?"

In reply I said, "Sir, actually, Mr. Mathur's son James is my best friend, but last night he didn't attend my calls, after that his phone showed switched off and I became worried about him, that is why today I had went his house to meet him, but when I reached his house's gate, the security guards of his house didn't allow me to go inside, so, in frustration, I did it."

Then the police officer said, "Now we will show you what real frustration is." Saying these words, they started beating me.

After 30 minutes, Mr. Mathur called on the police officer's phone and said that today you teach him a good lesson so that he never do, this thing again.

In response, the police officer said to him, "Sir, don't worry I will handle him."

When I heard all this, I understood that all these things were done by Mr. Mathur so that I can go away from James' life.

After that, the police officer repeatedly asked me the same question: "Why did you go to Mr. Mathur's house?"

And I also gave the same answer, that I went to meet my friend.

My parents came to release me but the police did not allow them to enter the police station.

The police started to continue beating me, at the same time the words came out of my mouth that please let me go so that I can save my friend's life.

When the police officer heard these words from me, he asked me, "What do you mean? Is your friend having some kind of problem?"

In reply I said, "Yes sir, my friend's life is in danger, please sir let me go."

When the police officer heard this, he thought that someone wanted to kill my friend so he asked me who wants to kill your friend, what is the danger to him?

In reply, I said, "Sorry, sir, I cannot tell you what is dangerous to him."

Upon hearing this, the police officer got angry and started beating me again and said that I know you want to kill your friend for his money.

I said again and again that there is no such thing but the officer did not listen to me and told the policemen to keep beating him till he told the truth.

The night went on like this. I didn't tell the policeman about James' addiction because I didn't want my friend to be jailed because of me.

17

CHAPTER SEVEN

The next day, in the morning, my parents and my old friend Jessica, came to the police station.

Actually I and Jessica became friends in high school, we started to like each other very much from our high school days.

After high school, Jessica went on to become a lawyer, after that, we never met, but sometimes we talked on the call.

Now Jessica had become a successful lawyer and she had come with my parents to pick me up from the police station.

After my bail, when I was taken out of lock-up I can't even walk on my own.

The police had beaten me so badly that I had wounds all over my body.

When Jessica and my parents saw me, they were shocked. My parents took me in Jessica's car.

After that Jessica said to my parents that you will go home, and I will take him to the hospital.

On the way, Jessica tried to talk to me but I didn't answer her, I just thought of my friend.

Then Jessica said that since we met, you haven't talked to me. I thought you would meet me and be happy but now I think you didn't have pleasure in meeting me.

On hearing this, I said, "No, there are no such things, actually I'm in trouble so I'm just thinking about it.

Then Jessica asked me, "Why you are so tense, your parents told me that your friend's father had arrested you by the police. Tell me, I will not tell anyone. I promise."

I didn't say anything at first when she asks, but when she started forced me I told her everything.

When she heard all this, she was very shocked and said, "Don't worry, I will also help you to find your friend."

After that, we reached the hospital. She took me inside the hospital and told the doctor to treat me.

We talked a lot all the way, when we are going home after treatment. At that time I forgot all the worries.

While talking, we didn't remind when we reached home.

Then she told me not to get tense, I will come to your house tomorrow and we will search for your friend together.

Jessica's words gave me some hope that I would be able to find my friend.

Saying this, she went to her house and I also went inside my house.

As I entered the house, I saw my parents waiting for me. They stood when they saw me. I can see clearly on their faces that they are very worried for me.

Noticing that, I decided I'm not going to do anything that would upset my parents.

I treated them as if I no longer had any tension. But I forgot that every parent knows everything about their child.

My whole body aches a lot from being beaten by the police.

After eating and taking medicine I felt sleepy, so I went to sleep in my room. When I got to my room, I saw a photo in which me and James were riding horses.

In fact, there were pictures of our and mine memories everywhere in my room.

One of these photos was with my bed.

I took it in my hand and hugged it and said, "Where are you my friend?"

Medicine makes me sleepy and I fall asleep.

The next day, I was waiting for Jessica but she didn't come. After waiting a few hours I decided that now I will go alone to find my friend.

As I left my room, the door to my room opened and I saw Jessica.

As soon as she entered the room, she looked at the pictures and was surprised to see them.

I told her, "Where have you been till now, from many hours I've been waiting for you."

In response, she said, "Forgive me, I had a little work to do, that is why I can't come till now."

Then we left the house to find out about James. From morning till evening, we tried to find out about him but we did not get any information about him.

I got hurt so much, then Jessica told me, not to be tense, we'll try again tomorrow.

Actually, Mr. Mathur knew that I will try to find James, that is why he created problems so that I will never know about him.

The next day we went to find out about James again but we didn't find any information about him that day.

We tried to find out about him at every airport, every place, but no one told us anything about him.

A month went on like this but we never knew anything about him.

I lost hope, I felt like I would never see my friend again.

Jessica was very supportive of me but she also seemed to think that we would never be able to find James.

After that, I felt very anxious because I know that James will take a high dose of drugs. After all, he was alone and he would not be able to escape from the drugs.

I got so tense that I always held his picture close to my chest, and started sharing my feelings with the picture

CHAPTER EIGHT

On the other hand, James also missed me a lot, and he also took my photo in his hand and talked to it. And he said to the photo, "My friend forgive me, I promised you that if the whole world left you, I would never leave you, but those drugs ruined my whole life, and I wouldn't want your life to be ruined just like me, that's why I couldn't support you."

And he said that I haven't had the love of my parents since I was a child, they have always been busy with their work.

From my childhood, I wanted to spend time with my parents and go on vacation with them like other children, but they never gave me time or understood my feelings.

When I started to feel that my parents did not love me then my quarrel with my parents started to grow day by day.

And one day I had a big fight with them which made me very sad, and that day I met a man who told me that you seemed very upset, I have something for you that will take away all your pains if you want I can give it to you.

I agreed with him and he gave me a packet of drugs.

The first time I started taking it, I felt like I forgot my pains, but after a few months, when I got used to it, my life started to get worse than before.

And he said, "My life has become like hell, I can't even leave it now, and these drugs are slowly ending my life."

I didn't know how long I would live but yes, as long as I live I will regret why I started it.

While talking, he fell into a deep sleep.

James got drunk all day because he was alone, when he moved to a new place he didn't know where to get drugs.

When he couldn't find drugs he started Alcohol instead.

He went to the bar every day to drink, and sometimes he drank so much that he fell asleep in the bar.

In the same way, as the days went by and one day he found a man in a bar who was known as Kalbi, the Dealer.

Kalbi was a very dangerous gangster, he did all kinds of wrong things, from drug dealing to dealing of girls, that's why people called him Kalbi, the Dealer.

When James was drunk he told Kalbi that he wanted drugs and he can do anything for drugs, then an idea came to Kalbi's mind that he would add James to his team by giving him drugs and making him do all the wrong things and if ever the police found out he would lay full blame on James.

Kalbi said, "Don't worry, I'll give you drugs, but for them, you have to work for me." At that time James only thought about drugs and said that he shall do anything for drugs, but he did not know that this decision would ruin his whole life.

After that, Kalbi gave him one mobile number and one packet of cocaine.

And said that when this packet of cocaine would be ended then you should call on this number, after that, I will tell you what to do next.

After telling all this, Kalbi left and James also went back to his hotel room.

After arriving in the room, he took a packet of cocaine out of his pocket and started taking it. He took high doses of It even though he was already drunk.

His whole body was trembling after taking drugs, his eyes became red, he felt very weak and started vomiting blood, but no longer minded or afraid of all these things, because he now knows that he will not be able to give up drugs, nor will he be able to survive.

A few days later when James's drug packet runs out, he calls the number given by Kalbi.

Kalbi picked up his call and then sent a location to James mobile.

When he arrived at the location, he saw nothing but an old factory.

After that, some servants came to pick up James and they took him inside the factory.

When he arrived inside the factory, he saw Kalbi and many others waiting for him.

When Kalbi looked at James, he offered him to sit on the chair, And said just like I told you before, I'll give you as many drugs as you want, but you'll have to do one thing for me.

When he heard this, he asked him to tell him what he has to do for drugs.

Then Kalbi told him that you have to take my truck somewhere with a lot of drugs in it but one thing to keep in mind is that no one could about it, and he said that if you did this work for me, I will give you as many drugs as you wanted, but one thing if this truck is seized by the police, my name shouldn't be included in all of them.

After hearing all this, James told Kalbi, "This is all wrong and that I will not do it."

After saying all this, James started to leave

And Kalbi started giving him more drugs and greed and said, "This is the only thing you have to do for me, then you will take your drugs and leave."

After hearing this, James finally agreed with him.

Then Kalbi told him to come here tomorrow morning and I would tell you where to deliver the goods.

And Kalbi gave him another packet of drugs and told to go get it and have fun tonight.

At that time James became convinced of Kalbi's words and he thought that this is the only thing he has to do. After that Kalbi will give him a lot of drugs, but he doesn't know how many lives Kalbi has ruined by telling such lies.

CHAPTER NINE

The next day James woke up and got ready to go, and when he got there, he saw that Kalbi was already waiting for him.

After that Kalbi gave him the keys of the truck and said that I would send you the location of that place on your number. You can go now and one thing is that my people will follow you, if something went wrong in your mind my people would shoot you.

When James heard this he got very scared and started the truck and went towards that place which was sent by Kalbi to him.

On their way, he saw that the police officers were checking all the cars, and then he called on Kalbi's mobile and said everything.

Kalbi called his men, who were following James, and told them to distract the police, so that James could deliver the goods safely.

They agreed with Kalbi and they distracted the police, and James found an opportunity and left from there.

He faced a lot of troubles on his way but finally, he safely delivered the drugs to the respective place.

Kalbi was very happy with this and he gave him more drugs and said that now you are my friend, you could call me whenever you need drugs.

By saying such sweet words, Kalbi persuaded James and put him in the wrong things.

At first it seemed wrong for James to do all this work, but sooner or later he too began to enjoy it, and thus he became the right hand of Kalbi.

In doing so, two years passed and James became one of the top criminals.

To save himself from the police he thought that he would go to India and will come back when all is well.

The next day he came to India. And that same day Jessica took me to the market and as soon as we got to the market I saw James in a blue car and I started chasing that car.

Jessica stopped me a lot and said it's a delusion of your eyes but I didn't listen to her and started chasing the car.

I saw the car going through the gate of James's house and I was convinced that It was not a delusion of my eyes.

Then I started yelling at James and was telling my friend to meet me only once.

As soon as James heard my voice, he ran to his room terrace and from there he saw me.

As soon as he saw me tears started rolling on his cheeks and he said in his mind, "My friend, what have you done with yourself because of me?"

When I didn't get an answer for a long time, I cried loudly, "Okay, I'll just sit there and wait for you until you meet me."

Having said that, I sat on a bench in front of the gate of his house.

James was hearing all this and he got very upset and he thought that if he met me I would not let him go back and it would make my life more difficult.

After a while Jessica also came and sat next to me and told me, "Enough is enough, Tony, come home with me now."

I disobeyed her and told her, "I won't go anywhere unless I talk to my friend."

Hearing this, Jessica said, "Which friend are you talking about? A friend who doesn't care if you're with him or not."

She added, "The friend who left you in this state, the friend who caused you this condition, Or a friend who thinks only of himself."

And she said, "Please Tony, come back home with me."

It made me very angry to hear all this and I angrily told her who are you to say such things about my friend.

I said, "You know, he's not just my friend, he's my brother and I will never let anyone say anything wrong about my brother."

In response she told me, I understand but you try to understand James, he was just pretending to be friends with you. And do you think that person even once tried to find out about you what his father did to you after he left?

I got angry when I heard this and I slapped her and said, "You just said too much about my friend but not anymore."

Jessica was hurt by this move of mine and she left without saying anything.

James saw all this happening and he considered himself responsible for it and said that I thought that after my departure everything would be fine in Tony's life, but he has ruined himself because of me.

It was late at night and I didn't know when I fell asleep on the bench.

My whole body was shivering due to the cold and when James saw it all, he realised that he was wrong and he thought if Tony can do so much to save my life. To save our friendship, then I couldn't give up drugs for us.

After thinking about all this, he decided to quit drugs and shall start a new life.

And then he came with a blanket for me, after putting the blanket on me he kissed me on the forehead and grabbed my feet and he wept and said, "My friend, you have done a lot for me and you have lost a lot. Forgive me." Crying like this, he also fell asleep there.

The next day as soon as my eyes opened I saw a blanket over me and I saw a man lying at my feet. And as soon as I picked him up, I found that the man was none other than James.

Tears welled up in my eyes as I looked at him. And I slapped him hard and grabbed him by the collar of his shirt and I said to him, "If you had to leave me alone, then why did you come into my life?"

In reply, he said, "I know that I have done wrong to you and now whatever punishment you give me will be accepted but please forgive me, I thought that if I stayed with you, your life would be ruined." "That is why I walked away from your life but now I realize how wrong I was. Please forgive me, my friend."

In reply, I said to him, "That you will surely be punished and your punishment is that you will have to make a solemn promise to me that you will not leave me alone anywhere."

Then he promised me that he would not leave me alone.

I was very happy to hear that because I was looking at the truth in his eyes at that time.

We both got emotional and hugged and kissed each other.

It seemed to me that I have finally regained my friend's friendship after so many difficulties and now I will not let my friend go anywhere but even then I was wrong. We didn't know that fate would strike us again.

We were talking to each other when Mr. Mathur saw us, he got very angry when he saw us like this and he came to us quickly and told me, "You are here again, I think you have forgotten the lesson of the last time, and I will have to remind you again and again, but at this time I will make sure that you do not get out of jail as easily as last time."

James didn't know all these things but when he heard these things from Mr. Mathur he was very upset and he said to Mr. Mathur, "Father, today I will tell you the truth, You've always misunderstood Tony, but he's not exactly what you think he is. He has always got me out of trouble and even this time, what he did was to save my life."

He added, "You always said bad things about him, but he never thought badly of our family and always protects our family."

Mr. Mathur was shocked to hear all this and he would realise all his mistakes, and he said to me, "Please forgive me for my mistakes, son. To this day it seemed to me that you are just after our money but I was wrong, you always saved my family. I should have thanked you, but I did all this to you, so forgive me, if you can."

In reply, I told him that I have never taken your words to heart and I have always considered your family as my own, and everything I've done so far has been done with my family in mind.

On hearing this, Mr. Mathur hugged me and said, "I don't have only one son from today but two beloved son's instead.

I became very happy to hear all this from him, Because I always thought that James ' family would accept me one day, and this is the day they accepted me.

After that day, James and I became very happy. We spent most of our time together, we had a lot of fun and our friendship grew stronger than ever.

CHAPTER TEN

One day, James and I were sitting in a park and he talked to me about Jessica and said, "You should go and apologize to her, because you didn't do well with her that day."

In response, I told him that she will not forgive me, because I have hurt her so much.

Then James said it's all happened because of me and I will fix it. He said, "Now we both go and apologize to her."

As soon as we got up to leave, James got dizzy and fell down. As soon as he falls down, blood starts coming from his mouth and nose, and his whole body starts trembling.

I carried him on my shoulder and put him in the car and rushed him to the hospital.

On the other hand, someone told this news to James' family and mine.

I was scared to see the condition of James, and I remembered the doctor saying that if your friend didn't stop taking drugs, he won't be able to survive. All these things were going on in my mind and finally we reached the hospital.

As soon as I got to the hospital, I talked to the doctors' and then they took James to I.C.U, and told me to wait outside.

I sat outside in the chair, and after a while I saw that his family with my family were coming there.

Seeing all of them, I got very emotional and started hugging, Mr. Mathur and my father and I wept and told them the whole truth about how James got addicted to drugs and what happened to us after that.

They were very surprised to hear this and comforted me and said, "Not to be tense, James will be fine. Now we have come and we will not let anything happen to him."

We all started waiting outside the I.C.U, and after some hours the doctor came out of the I.C.U, noticing the doctor Mr. Mathur asked him, "How is my son now?"

The doctor told him, "He is out of danger right now, but he has spread cancer all over his body."

In other words Doctors will only be able to keep him alive for a few days.

We all were shocked to heard these words of the doctor and Mr. Mathur said to the doctor that, "I will bring good doctors from around the world for my son."

The doctor, in response, told Mr.Mathur, "That there is not any doctor who can do it now, because James' cancer is at a last stage. And if we had known about it earlier, we might have saved him, but nothing can be done now. It is impossible to save him now."

"Forgive me," he said and left.

Hearing these words, we all got shocked, all believed the words of the doctor and started crying. But I still don't believe in all that, and I cried and said, "No, it's all a lie, my friend can't do that to me, he promised me he would never go anywhere again leaving me alone and he can't break his promise to me, I won't let him go anywhere."

Viewing my condition, everyone started comforting me, and in the middle a nurse came and said that you all have been called in by the patient.

When we all went in, James called his parents first and said, "Father, Mother, forgive me because I didn't understand you. You've been busy with your work since I was a kid and it made me feel like you didn't care me, you didn't love me, I wanted to understood you that whatever you were doing, you were doing it for me, but I started hating you and that's why I went stray and got involved in wrong things. Forgive me if you can because I could not be your good son."

In response, James's parents said, "No, son, forgive us. We were beginning to think our work was so important, due to which we never thought about you, that it is important to give you time."

James then told my parents, "Uncle, aunty, please forgive me because I know I've unknowingly shown you a lot of troubles."

Then James said, "Tony, my friend, come and sit next to me."

I listened to him and sat next to him.

He took my hand and said to me, "My friend, I have no right to apologize to you."

Since childhood, I have received the love of brother, friend and parents from you. You have done a lot for me till today, but I have only caused you pain and suffering till now.

You always supported me in my difficult times, you tried very hard and even explained to me that I should stop taking drugs, but I didn't listen to any of your advice and look! These drugs are taking my life today, my friend.

I listened to him, hugged him, and said, "I will not let anything happen to you, my friend."

In response, he said, "That the doctor has told me everything, and now I know that I will soon leave this world and all of you and go away forever."

Hearing this from him, I got very emotional and ran out of the I.C.U. Going out, I started crying and said, "My friend, I can't see you die. I wish I will die instead of you and you will be saved."

Everyone came out after hearing my crying and said to me, "Tony, go in now, he needs you the most, and if you give up like that, who's going to take care of him."

I obeyed them, almost with tears I went inside, and in the meantime the doctor also came there, and I asked the doctor when we could take James back home.

In reply he told me that James's condition would get worse day by day, so I can't allow him to be taken home.

After hearing this, we all begged the doctor to please let James go with us, but he didn't listen to us.

Then James asked the doctor how many more days longer I have left.

In disappointment, the doctor replied that it's only a week.

Hearing this, James said, "Please, doctor, let me go home with them, because I want to spend the last week of my life with them".

This time the doctor couldn't deny James' request and said he's ok. If that's what you want, I will give permission, but I'll still send some of my staff with you to take care of you.

Then we all thanked the Doctor. He takes us away from James and said I was sending James home with you tomorrow, But you all have to take care of one thing that no one would cry in front of him, you all have to try to keep him happy as much as possible, because if he starts to be sad, his condition may become worse than before.

In reply, we all say, "Ok, doctor, we will take special care of that thing."

I was devastated by the switch that my friend would only be with us for a week and after that my friend would leave us forever.

I was sitting next to James and I was thinking all these things and meanwhile James said to me, "Tonny, I want to spend the last days of my life with you and I want to do everything that makes you happy."

Hearing this, I held his hand and said, "Brother, I will not let you go anywhere and now you stop thinking about all these things and do the rest."

After eating, when James took the medicine, he started to feel sleepy and fell asleep. After he went to bed, I told everyone to go home and rest. "Don't stress, I'll stay here to take care of James." I said.

At first they all didn't listen to me. But then finally, after my insistence, they accepted my words and went home.

After that, I stayed with James all night and took care of him.

CHAPTER ELEVEN

The next day, as soon as James was discharged from the hospital he told his family and mine to go home and said, "Tony and I have some work to do, we'll be right back."

Then I told him, "James, we go home first and rest then we will go where we need to go." But he didn't listen to me and said, "Come with me, I have to introduce you to someone."

I agreed with him and got ready to go with him.

After that we both sat in the car and left. On the way, I asked James a lot about where we are going but he didn't tell me anything.

After walking for 10 km, James stopped the car and told me to get out of the car.

As I got out of the car, I saw that we were in front of a restaurant and then James told me to come in with me.

James has invited Jessica there since the first and when I saw Jessica after entering the restaurant I was surprised and asked James what is all this?

In reply, he said that I have called him here so that we can talk and everything will be fine as before.

After that we went and sat down with Jessica and she asked James why you called me here.

In response, James told her, "Look, listen to me carefully. It's not Tony's fault, it's my fault." And whatever he did, he did it for me and I would never want you two to be apart because of me. And I promise he will never do that to you again, "Please forgive him today."

In response Jessica said that I will never be able to forgive him for that and anyway this didn't want anyone else but you.

James then said I know, he loves me the most in the whole world and I love him too, and I know you were the only one who could take care of him after I was gone.

Hearing this, Jessica laughed, and said, "You are his friend, first you falsely claim to love him and then you always leave him alone."

Hearing Jessica's words, I got angry and left in anger because I didn't want to say anything else in anger at that time.

When Jessica saw this, she said it's enough; I didn't come here to do my disrespect, now I'm going home.

In response, James told her, first, listen to me clearly and he said that I'm not making any false claims and first I left Tony alone because I didn't want him to ruin his life because of me. And now I don't want to leave Tony alone but my illness won't let me.

Jessica heard this and said, "What disease? Who are you talking about?"

Distraught, James replied that I have the last-stage of cancer and the doctors said that I only have a week to live.

Jessica was shocked to hear this and said, "Forgive me, I didn't know all this and I said all this in anger."

James said, "No problem," and he said, "You take care of Tony after I left and I know you are the only one who can take care of him. Because after I leave this world, Tony will be completely broken and alone, and I want you to give him so much happiness after me, so that he can forget me easily."

In response Jessica said, "I didn't know all this and I can never take your place in Tony's life and neither can anyone else. But I will still try my best".

Hearing this James said, "Thank you very much, I know you will take good care of him and now I can leave this world in peace."

Then James said we should go now, Tony will be waiting for us, saying that they both came out.

After coming out, Jessica came to me and said, "I'm sorry, I said something stupid, I shouldn't have said it."

In response, I said, "No problem, forgive me as well, I have not treated you well either."

Then Jessica said, "Come on! It's too late, you both go home and I go home too".

James asked her also to "come with us, we will leave you at your home.

Then we all sat in the car. Along the way, James and I talked to Jessica about our childhood. And in the meantime we don't know when we have reached Jessica's house.

After dropping Jessica off at her house, we both came home. Everyone was waiting for us at James's house, and when they saw us, they said, "Where did you two take so long?"

In response, James said that he had met an old friend, so time was spent with him.

Then I told James, you should rest now, brother, and I took him to his room and laid him down on the bed, and I also sat with him.

James rested his head on my shoulder. I felt so happy at that moment and I wished we could just stay together.

After a while I also fall asleep like this.

James's condition started to deteriorate day by day and he became very weak, with dark circles under his eyes.

CHAPTER TWELVE

Days passed by and finally the day came which I never wanted to think about.

As usual, we were spending time together and James said to me, "Brother, I don't feel good here, why don't we go out somewhere and also take Jessica with us?"

I didn't agree with him and told him, "No, not today, next time, now you just have to rest." But he didn't listen to me and forced me a lot and said, "Please accept my request."

Viewing him forcing me, his parents told me that if James insists, you hang around a bit and he will like it.

I obeyed them and went with James. We picked up Jessica on the way and we went to our favorite place, which is on the bank of a river, where only the beauty of nature can be seen.

I told Jessica that this place has a lot of childhood memories for me and James. We used to spend time together here whenever we were very sad.

Jessica then said that really this place is very beautiful and from today this place has become my favorite too.

Then the three of us sat there, enjoying each other's fun and nature, while James vomited blood from his mouth. He doesn't even have the courage to talk to us anymore, and he started having trouble breathing.

Jessica and I got scared and rushed him to the hospital as fast as we could.

After that, Doctor's, once again admitted James to the I.C.U and we also called everyone to the hospital.

They arrived at the hospital and then we all started praying for James that nothing should happen to him and that he will be fine.

At that time I was crying a lot for James and looking at me, Jessica tried to comfort me and said, "Don't worry, nothing will happen to him."

In a tearful reply, I said, "You know that once I lost my friend, and now after much difficulty I have got my friend back, I don't have enough courage left in me to lose my friend's friendship again. Now I will not be able to live without my friend."

Jessica got emotional listening to me and tears started rolling from her eyes too.

After a while the I.C.U lights turned off and the doctor came out of the I.C.U disappointed and said, us to forgive us,

We did our best to save James's life in whatever way we could, but we did not found any way to save him.

And he added now his condition is such that he can die at any moment.

Hearing this from the doctor, it was as if the ground was torn from under our feet.

We all started crying, I got dizzy and I fell to the ground.

Then they also entered me in another ward.

As soon as I regained consciousness, I saw Jessica sitting next to me.

I asked her where the others are?

In response she said, they are sitting next to James.

Then I said I also have to go to my friend. And I got out of bed to go.

Then the nurse came there and said, "You need a lot of rest, you can't go anywhere."

But I didn't listen to her and told Jessica to please take me to my friend.

Jessica took me to James's ward and I saw everyone crying and James in so much pain, he was filling his list of breaths. I got very emotional viewing all this and freeing Jessica's hand, I ran to James and gave him a big hug and cried a lot.

James was having trouble talking and breathing. But still he told me, "Brother, I was waiting for you, because I wanted to see and talk to my friend one last time before I leave this world. And now I can die in peace."

Hearing his words, I said, "I will not let you go anywhere."

Then he said, "Tony, I will always be with you even after I leave this world and I will always be a star watching you from the sky. And when you see me at night, I will always shine when I see you."

And he also added, "Please stop crying now, because I want you to say goodbye to me with a smile. And promise me that you will be a good doctor and you will be aware and treat drug-affected people like me, so that no one else ends up wasting their lives like me."

Then he called Jessica to him and told her, "Take care of my friend after I left, And I want you to promise me today that you will take care and accompany my friend in the same way."

While saying this, his breath stopped and he died in my arms.

That week was the best and worst week of my life. Good because my friend was with me again and worst because after that week my friend is separated from me forever.

It hurts me a lot after parting with my friend, but I also have to fulfill the promise I made to him, so I worked hard and finally became a good doctor.

After becoming a doctor, I did more research on drugs and started my own NGO, in which I went from place to place and explained to people how drugs ruin lives.

I will never have a friend like James and I will always miss him. And even today, when I miss James, I go to the open sky and look at the stars. And whenever I do that, always one of those stars shines bright on viewing me. And then I talk to him.

Even today, I am very sad that if my friend had not studied drugs, he would have been with me today.

Finally, I will just say that drugs not only ruin our lives, but they also ruin the lives of our loved ones.

This is what is happening in our environment today that we are getting involved in drugs especially the young generation.

Whenever we get into a problem, we should reconcile with our loved ones and try to fight the problem.

If we are afraid of this problem and give up, we will do something by which we will ruin our own life and that of our family.

And if ever the idea of taking drugs comes to your mind, then you must think once about those people who love you the most, what effect it will have on them.

Thank you